In the Pouch

Written by Michèle Dufresne

PIONEER VALLEY EDUCATIONAL PRESS, INC.

Some **animals** have a **pouch**.

A pouch is a flap of skin.

A small **joey** can nap, ride, or hide

in its mother's pouch.

Some animals that have pouches are called marsupials. The pouch is called a marsupium (maar-**soo**-pee-uhm).

This is a **kangaroo**.

A mother kangaroo has a pouch.

As the mother hops here

and there, a joey can ride

in her pouch.

The joey is safe by her side.

A kangaroo joey lives in
its mother's pouch for
about six months.

This is a **wallaby**.

The joey can jump in

and out of its mother's pouch.

A wallaby likes to munch on grass
and plants.
Its big back legs help
it hop fast for many miles.

Here is a **koala**.

Koalas also have a pouch.

They are white and **gray**.

Koalas like to take long naps.

Koalas are not bears, even though they look like cute teddy bears. They are marsupials. They eat eucalyptus leaves and sleep up to 18 hours a day.

8

Here is a **Tasmanian devil.**

Tasmanian devils are black.

They are the size of a small dog.

They have a big, big bite.

Tasmanian devils have strong jaws and sharp teeth that can crush bones and pull apart meat.

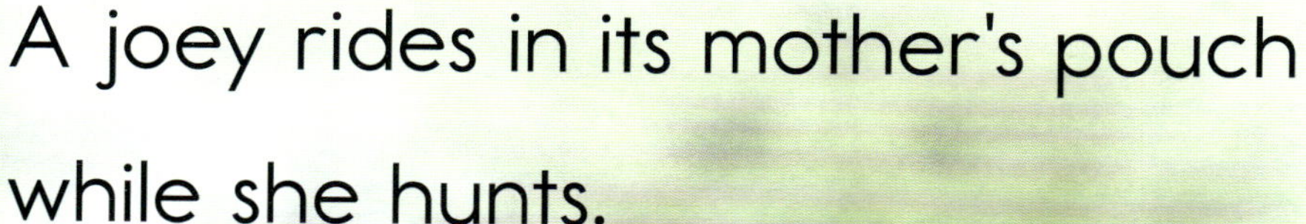

A joey rides in its mother's pouch while she hunts.

Baby Tasmanian devils grow fast and leave the pouch after about 100 days. Sometimes they go back in to be safe.

glossary

animals:
living things
that move, eat,
and grow

gray:
a color that is
a mix of black
and white

joey:
a baby animal
that grows in its
mother's pouch

kangaroo:
a large animal
with strong hind
legs that hops and
carries its baby in
a pouch

koala:
a gray animal
that lives in trees,
eats leaves, and
carries its baby
in a pouch

pouch:
a flap of skin on
a mother's body
where her baby
can ride, hide, eat,
and grow

Tasmanian devil:
a small animal
with sharp teeth
that has a pouch
and lives on
the island
of Tasmania

wallaby:
a small animal
that looks like a
kangaroo, has a
pouch, and hops